THIS WALKER BOOK BELONGS TO:

_____

_____

_____

_____

For Albert

With thanks to John Barker, B. Vet. Med., M.R.C.V.S.

First published 1982 by Evans Brothers Ltd
First published 1991 by
Walker Books Ltd, 87 Vauxhall Walk
London SE11 5HJ

This edition published 1996

2 4 6 8 10 9 7 5 3 1

© 1982, 1996 Colin Hawkins

This book has been typeset in Monotype Garamond.

Printed in Hong Kong
British Library Cataloguing in Publication Data
A catalogue record for this book is
available from the British Library.

ISBN 0-7445-4737-7

How to Look After Your CAT

Colin and Jacqui Hawkins

WALKER BOOKS
AND SUBSIDIARIES

LONDON • BOSTON • SYDNEY

Which Cat?

What kind of cat
would you like to own?
Should it be male or female?

If you decide on a female
would you like her
to have kittens?

Should it be a long-haired
or a short-haired cat?

Long-haired cats are very
beautiful animals but require
a great deal of grooming.

Siamese cats are affectionate
and playful, but they can be
destructive and noisy.

"What a beautiful pussy I am."

"I'm noisy but fun."

"Didn't I do well!"

Silliest cat of the show

The Cornish Rex has crinkled fur and whiskers.

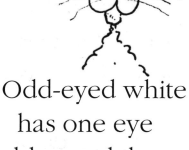

"And I've got a crinkly tail."

Odd-eyed white has one eye blue and the other orange.

Would you prefer an exotic cat who can be entered for cat shows, but who will be expensive to buy and maintain, or a cross-bred cat who will be cheap to buy and possibly healthier and stronger?

"I'm a hardy chap."

If you are adopted by a stray cat, take her to the vet to check she's healthy.

Choosing Your Cat

In selecting a healthy kitten look for the following:

clean ears

clear, bright eyes

alert, happy nature

damp, moist nose

healthy, pink tongue

sleek, well-groomed coat

strong, firm limbs and feet

licked clean.

a good appetite

Avoid overweight kittens.
They could have a glandular
problem. Pick a lively,
happy kitten.

It is best to get a kitten
from a friend or breeder, so that
you can see the whole litter with their mother.

Shy, nervous, hissing kittens
do not make good pets.

Sneezing
kittens should
also be avoided
as they may well
have asthmatic problems or even cat flu.

The New Kitten

You should take your new pet to the vet as soon as possible. She will need worming and must be vaccinated against flu, enteritis and leukaemia at nine and twelve weeks old.

Kittens should not be taken away from their mother before they have been weaned at six to eight weeks old.

"You mean it's all mine?"

Provide the new kitten with her own basket.

Keep your kitten indoors for at least six days so that she can become familiar with her new home.

Make sure she has a litter tray, indoors to start with.

It can gradually be moved closer to the door …

and then eventually outside.

Diet

Do not over-feed your kitten. She is an enthusiastic eater and will literally eat until she is sick.

"I don't feel well..."

Kittens should have four small meals a day until they are twelve weeks old then you can reduce to two. Cats will enjoy fresh cooked fish or chicken, but your pet will have a perfectly balanced diet if you give her tinned or dried food.

Make sure your cat has fresh water to drink at all times. Some cats drink tea, but never give them milk as it can cause diarrhoea.

"More tea, Tiddles?"

"Yes, please Bodger. Helps keep the old coat in trim."

Never put your plate on the floor for your cat to finish off any scraps or she may begin to steal from the table.

Cats need to eat grass. It helps their digestion and prevents hair-balls forming after grooming.

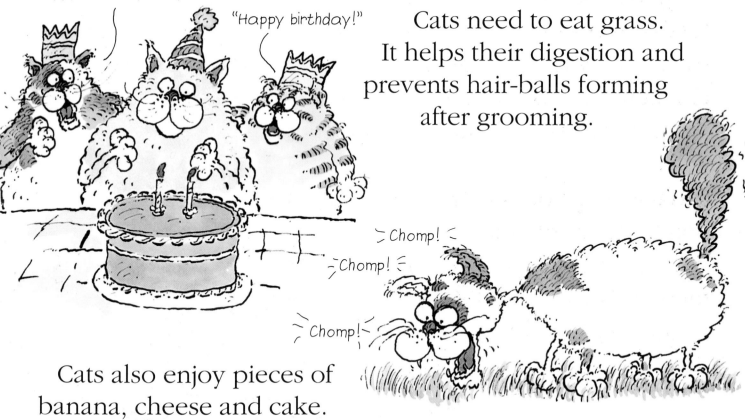

Cats also enjoy pieces of banana, cheese and cake.

Grooming

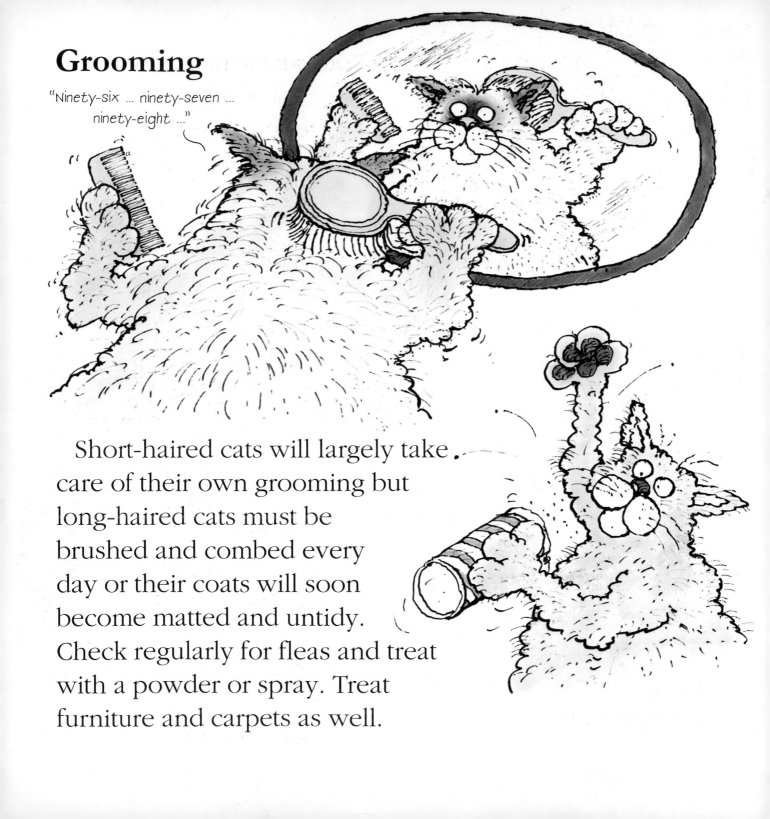

"Ninety-six ... ninety-seven ... ninety-eight ..."

Short-haired cats will largely take care of their own grooming but long-haired cats must be brushed and combed every day or their coats will soon become matted and untidy. Check regularly for fleas and treat with a powder or spray. Treat furniture and carpets as well.

"Keeps away the tooth decay."

You can clean a cat's teeth with a soft cloth and salt water but dried food will also help keep teeth clean and strong.

"We are not amused."

Cats hate being bathed and should only be given a bath in extreme situations. Use only warm water with a mild soap, avoid disinfectants, and then rinse and dry very well.

Keep her indoors until she is completely dry.

Cat Care

Provide a secure and well-ventilated cat basket when transporting your cat over any distance.

Cats as a rule do not enjoy travelling, so make the basket as warm and comfortable as possible.

"Are we there yet?"

"Marvellous things, elasticated collars."

It's a good idea for a cat to wear a collar that can carry her name and address. Do make sure that it is elasticated.

A bell attached to a collar will help to prevent a cat from catching birds and mice.

"Bother that bell!"

('Ding!

Ding!')

A flap fitted to an outside door will allow your cat to come and go as she wishes. Although you can have the occasional unexpected visitor.

Providing your cat with a scratching post can prevent damage to furniture.

Take your cat to the vet if her nails need trimming.

Sick Cats and How to Recognize Them

"Same old boring muck!"

Loss of appetite

This may simply mean that she is bored with her diet. Try changing it.

Shivering

"Is it cold or is it me?"

"I knew I shouldn't have eaten those pilchards or the chicken or the tripe..."

Being sick

This may be due to overeating.

"Look, you've got a hot, dry nose!"

A hot, dry nose

Sneezing

Cat flu can be very dangerous. The occasional sneezing fit however is more likely to be due to dust or hay fever.

"Atishoo!"

"You should see the other cat!"

Bald patches

These can be a sign of ringworm or a vitamin deficiency. Or may be due to fighting. Patches on the neck may be caused by the collar rubbing.

"I'm suffering from at least four of these symptoms. Take me to a vet, quick!"

Cats are creatures of habit and any unusual behaviour might be a sign that you should take her to the vet.

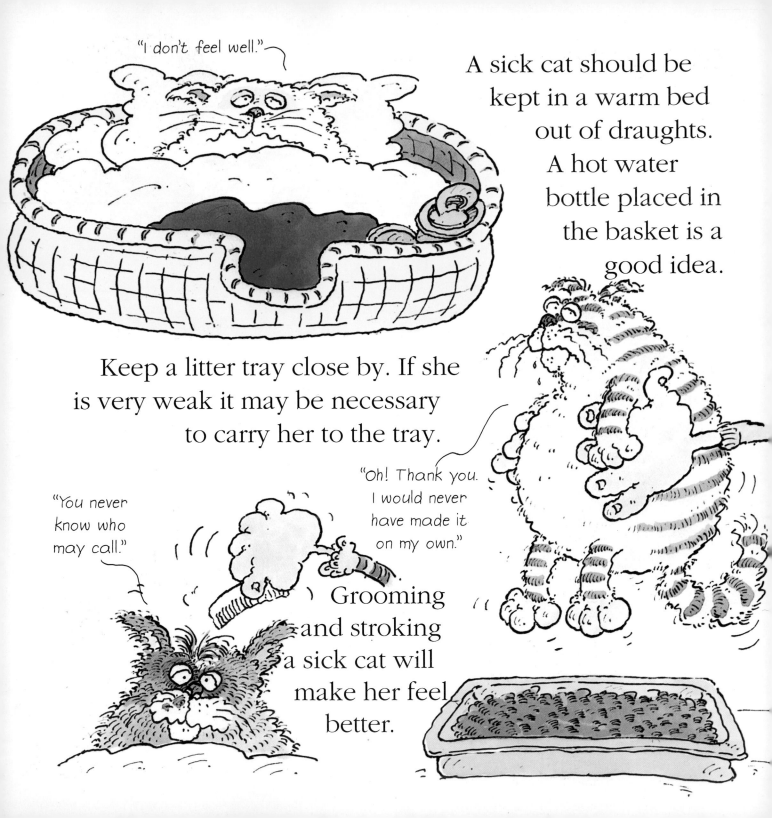

"I don't feel well."

A sick cat should be kept in a warm bed out of draughts. A hot water bottle placed in the basket is a good idea.

Keep a litter tray close by. If she is very weak it may be necessary to carry her to the tray.

"Oh! Thank you. I would never have made it on my own."

"You never know who may call."

Grooming and stroking a sick cat will make her feel better.

Giving Tablets

To stop your cat from spitting a tablet out, make sure that you place it right at the back of her tongue and then hold her mouth closed until she swallows. Wrapping her in a towel will make her easy to hold and stop her trying to scratch you.

Kittens or Not?

You should decide if you want your cat to be sterilized before he or she is six months old.

"I said, get off my roof!"

"A quick spray."

Unsterilized male cats will fight other male cats over territorial rights. They will also mark their territory with very pungent urine.

It is often thought that sterilized male cats become fat and lazy. A cat will only become fat and lazy if over-fed.

"Mice are such sweet little things."

"Stupid cat!"

"Hello, boys."

When in season, a female cat will attract gangs of enthusiastic and raucous suitors.

"And did you know that we are all pregnant again?"

An unsterilized female cat will come into season three times a year. Unless you are able to find homes for all her kittens you will soon have a very large family of cats to feed.

The Mother-To-Be

"Fifty-seven ... fifty-eight ... any day now..."

"Good grief! Look at the size of that cat!"

A cat's pregnancy lasts between sixty and sixty-five days. During the final twenty-one days she will become very large indeed.

"It's very nice, but I'll just add some fur..."

Just before she has the kittens she will become restless and begin looking for a suitable place to have her litter. When she has found the right spot, make it comfortable for her with blankets or newspapers.

Try to prevent her from being frightened late in her pregnancy or she may miscarry.

She may need to eat and drink more frequently.

Shortly before the birth she will become incredibly affectionate.

The Happy Event

It is very important to avoid disturbing the new mother or she may carry off the kittens to a more inaccessible place.

A mother cat will eat at least four times more than she normally eats.

At about two weeks, place a litter tray near the bed. The mother cat will then teach the kittens how to use it.

The kittens can start to be weaned at about three weeks.

They will learn how to drink by trial and error.

Kittens will begin to lose their milk teeth at about four months.

Kittens will open their eyes after about nine days, but it will be two or three more days before they are able to hear.

Cat Tales

All American tabby cats are thought to be descended from the ship's cat that came over with the Pilgrim Fathers.

We probably call our cats "puss" after the Eygptian cat goddess "Pasht".

"It's really good being a god."

"I'm a Pilgrim Pussy."

"O Holy Puss!"

"He's a god, you know!"

"Well, fancy that."

In Australia thirteen kittens were born in one litter – and they all survived.

Turkish Van cats actually enjoy swimming and will spend long periods of time in the water.

In Mexico there is a breed of cat without any hair.

MORE WALKER PAPERBACKS
For You to Enjoy

Also by Colin & Jacqui Hawkins

HOW TO LOOK AFTER YOUR...

Four brilliant pet-care books, packed with information for the young, would-be pet owner.

"A must… There are useful tips on home, feeding, health
and much more with fun drawings." *R.S.P.C.A. Animal Action*

How to Look After Your Cat   0-7445-4737-7
How to Look After Your Dog   0-7445-4738-5
How to Look After Your Hamster   0-7445-4379-7
How to Look After Your Rabbit   0-7445-4380-0
£4.50 each

COME FOR A RIDE ON THE GHOST TRAIN

"Every page must be turned with care as a comic, but wholly
scary surprise is revealed under the simplest flaps. Irresistible."
Julia Eccleshare, The Bookseller

0-7445-3671-5   £4.99

TERRIBLE TERRIBLE TIGER/THE WIZARD'S CAT

Two wonderfully entertaining rhyming picture books about a tiger
who is not quite what he seems and a cat who wishes he were something else!

Terrible Terrible Tiger   0-7445-1063-5   £3.99
The Wizard's Cat   0-7445-1389-8   £2.99